ALEXANDRIA OCASIO-CORTEZ
Making a Difference in Politics

By Katie Kawa

KidHaven
PUBLISHING

People Who Make a Difference

Published in 2021 by
KidHaven Publishing, an Imprint of Greenhaven Publishing, LLC
353 3rd Avenue
Suite 255
New York, NY 10010

Designer: Deanna Paternostro
Editor: Katie Kawa

Photo credits: Cover Erik McGregor/Pacific Press/LightRocket via Getty Images; p. 5 lev radin/Shutterstock.com; p. 7 Erin Lefevre/NurPhoto via Getty Images; p. 9 Drew Angerer/Getty Images; p. 11 Aleksandr Dyskin/Shutterstock.com; p. 13 Scott Heins/Getty Images; p. 15 (main) Saul Loeb/AFP via Getty Images; p. 15 (inset) Alex Wroblewski/Getty Images; p. 17 (main) Alex Wong/Getty Images; p. 17 (inset) Aurora Samperio/NurPhoto via Getty Images; pp. 18, 20 Andrew Harrer/Bloomberg via Getty Images; p. 21 T.Sumaetho/Shutterstock.com.

Library of Congress Cataloging-in-Publication Data

Names: Kawa, Katie, author.
Title: Alexandria Ocasio-Cortez : making a difference in politics / Katie
  Kawa.
Other titles: Making a difference in politics
Description: First edition. | New York : KidHaven Publishing, [2021] |
  Series: People who make a difference | Includes bibliographical
  references and index.
Identifiers: LCCN 2019052388 (print) | LCCN 2019052389 (ebook) | ISBN
  9781534534704 (library binding) | ISBN 9781534534681 (paperback) | ISBN
  9781534534711 (ebook) | ISBN 9781534534698 (set)
Subjects: LCSH: Ocasio-Cortez, Alexandria, 1989–Juvenile literature. |
  Women legislators–United States–Biography–Juvenile literature. |
  Legislators–United States–Biography–Juvenile literature. | United
  States. Congress. House–Biography–Juvenile literature.
Classification: LCC E901.1.O27 K39 2021 (print) | LCC E901.1.O27 (ebook)
  | DDC 328.73/092 [B]–dc23
LC record available at https://lccn.loc.gov/2019052388
LC ebook record available at https://lccn.loc.gov/2019052389

Printed in the United States of America

Some of the images in this book illustrate individuals who are models. The depictions do not imply actual situations or events.

CPSIA compliance information: Batch #BS20K: For further information contact Greenhaven Publishing LLC, New York, New York at 1-844-317-7404.

Please visit our website, www.greenhavenpublishing.com. For a free color catalog of all our high-quality books, call toll free 1-844-317-7404 or fax 1-844-317-7405.

Find us on

CONTENTS

A NEW VOICE IN POLITICS

It can take a long time for change to happen in the world of politics, which deals with the government and ideas about how it should work. However, sometimes one person can make a big difference.

In 2018, Alexandria Ocasio-Cortez became a powerful new figure in politics when she was elected to the U.S. House of Representatives, which is part of Congress—the lawmaking branch of the U.S. government. She was the youngest woman ever elected to Congress, and she became a strong voice for new ideas in Washington, D.C. Her path to political success shows that, with hard work, anything's possible!

In Her Words

"I think that change is a lot closer than we think."

— Interview with *TIME* magazine from March 2019

Alexandria Ocasio-Cortez, who's sometimes known as AOC, had just turned 29 years old when she was elected to Congress. She's much younger than many other lawmakers, but she's shown that you're never too young to make a difference in the world around you.

GROWING UP IN NEW YORK

Alexandria Ocasio-Cortez was born on October 13, 1989. She spent her early childhood in a part of New York City called the Bronx. Then, her family moved to a different part of New York called Yorktown, which had better schools for her and her brother. Alexandria has said that seeing the difference between the Bronx and Yorktown showed her that where someone lives can often **affect** the opportunities they have to succeed. This made her want to help people in places like the Bronx.

Alexandria went to college in Boston, Massachusetts. During this time, she worked for a U.S. senator named Ted Kennedy and learned about politics.

In Her Words

"Women like me aren't supposed to run for office. I wasn't born to a wealthy or powerful family—mother from Puerto Rico, dad from the South Bronx … Going into politics wasn't in the plan."

— Ad posted on Twitter in May 2018

Alexandria's mother was born in Puerto Rico, and Alexandria is proud of where her family comes from. She's spoken out about issues that affect the people of Puerto Rico.

HARD TIMES

Life wasn't always easy for Alexandria. In 2008, her father died. She needed to help her family pay their bills, so she worked as a bartender and waitress.

Alexandria also started working with young people from the Latinx community in New York after college. The Latinx community is a group of people from Latin American backgrounds. However, this job didn't pay a lot, and she had to pay back her student loans—money she borrowed to pay for college. She started working more hours as a bartender and waitress to help pay her bills. This taught her a lot about the problems many Americans are facing.

In Her Words

"I find it **revealing** when people … say they're going to 'send me back to waitressing,' as if that is bad … It's as though they think being a member of Congress makes you … 'better' than a waitress. But our job is to serve, not rule."

— Tweet from March 8, 2019

In May 2019, Alexandria went back to a New York restaurant to work as a bartender and waitress again. This time, she was doing it to raise awareness. She wants to change the law so people who have these kinds of jobs are paid more. Fair pay is an issue that's very important to her.

CAUSES TO CARE ABOUT

Alexandria was soon **inspired** by U.S. senator Bernie Sanders, who was running for president in 2016. She wanted to help him get elected, so she **volunteered** for his campaign.

Bernie Sanders didn't become the president, but that didn't stop Alexandria from wanting to get more involved with issues she cared about. Next, she traveled to the Standing Rock Reservation, which is located in North Dakota and South Dakota. She joined the Native Americans who lived there in fighting the construction of an oil pipeline that would go through their land. She also visited Flint, Michigan, and learned about the city's problems with unhealthy drinking water.

In Her Words

"I think the me that walked out of that was … more open to taking **risks**."

— Interview with *TIME* magazine from March 2019 (speaking about her trip to Standing Rock)

Alexandria Ocasio-Cortez and Bernie Sanders share many beliefs about politics. For example, they both call themselves democratic socialists, which means they believe in a kind of government that gives workers more control over the **economy** and helps everyday people more than big businesses.

THE FIRST STEP

After Alexandria got back from the Standing Rock Reservation, she was asked about running for Congress to **represent** the Bronx and another part of New York called Queens. She believed this was the best way to help her community. First, she had to win the primary election—a smaller election to decide who represents their political group, or party, in the general election. She ran against Joe Crowley, who'd served in Congress for a long time, so many people didn't think she'd win.

However, Alexandria believed in herself. Her volunteers believed too. They worked hard, and it paid off. Alexandria won the primary in June 2018.

In Her Words

"You have given this country hope ... that when you knock on your neighbor's door, when you come to them with love, when you let them know that no matter your stance you are there for them—that we can make change."

— Speech to supporters after winning the primary election in June 2018

Alexandria's win in the primary made her famous! People from all over the country started talking about her new ideas for the Democratic Party.

WOMEN IN THE HOUSE

Alexandria won the primary, but she still needed to win the general election. She did this on November 6, 2018. Alexandria's win was one of many that changed what Congress looked like. In fact, when Alexandria officially became a member of Congress in January 2019, she was part of a record number of women of color in the House of Representatives.

Alexandria spent time with three other women of color who were new members of Congress: Ilhan Omar, Ayanna Pressley, and Rashida Tlaib. They became known as "the Squad." They've stood by each other, especially when other people have said unkind things about them.

In Her Words

"Justice is about making sure that being polite is not the same thing as being quiet. In fact, oftentimes, the most **righteous** thing you can do is shake the table."

— Speech at the 2019 Women's March in New York City

"the Squad"

Alexandria sometimes wears all-white outfits, such as the one she wore when she officially became a member of the House of Representatives. This is a way for her to honor the women who fought for the right to vote and who ran for office before her. These women often wore white too.

THE GREEN NEW DEAL

Alexandria got to work right away in Congress. After only a month in Washington, D.C., she and Senator Ed Markey worked together on a plan they called the Green New Deal. Part of the Green New Deal calls for creating new jobs and helping all Americans earn a living wage.

The most famous part of the Green New Deal, though, involves helping the **environment**. The Green New Deal calls for the United States to stop using fossil fuels, such as coal, oil, and natural gas. Alexandria cares a lot about fighting **climate change**, which is why she's fighting for the Green New Deal.

In Her Words

"We cannot **compromise** on saving our planet. We can't compromise on saving kids ... We have to do these things. If we want to do them in different ways, that's fine. But we can't not do them."

— Interview with *TIME* magazine from March 2019

Laws like the Green New Deal have to be voted on in Congress before they're passed, so lawmakers like Alexandria have to work hard to get people to agree with their plans. It can take a long time before ideas like the Green New Deal become actual laws.

GREEN NEW DEAL NOW

GREEN NEW DEAL

17

WORKING HARD

Alexandria has also fought for many other causes. She's worked to help **immigrants** and to call attention to problems with the ways they're treated. She's also questioned powerful people in hearings, holding them **accountable** for their actions. For example, in October 2019, she questioned Facebook cofounder Mark Zuckerberg about fake news on Facebook.

Social media—the collection of websites and apps that allows people to create online communities—has played a big part in Alexandria's life and work. She uses it to help people understand how the government works. She also uses it to give people a look at her life outside of Congress.

In Her Words

"There is never any fight that is too big for us to pick."

— Speech to supporters after winning the general election in November 2018

The Life of Alexandria Ocasio-Cortez

1989
Alexandria Ocasio-Cortez is born on October 13.

2008
Alexandria's father dies.

2016
Alexandria works as a volunteer for Bernie Sanders's presidential campaign.

Alexandria travels to Flint, Michigan, and the Standing Rock Reservation.

2017
Alexandria announces she's running for the House of Representatives.

2018
Alexandria wins the Democratic primary in June and the general election in November, becoming the youngest woman ever elected to the House of Representatives.

2019
Alexandria officially becomes a member of the House of Representatives in January.

Alexandria and Ed Markey announce their Green New Deal plan in February.

Alexandria questions Mark Zuckerberg about Facebook's problems in October.

2020
Alexandria runs for re-election to the House of Representatives.

Alexandria hasn't been involved in politics for very long, but she's been very busy!

FIGHTING FOR THE FUTURE

Alexandria believes in the power young people have to stand up for what they believe in. She's often said that she's working to make the future brighter for young people—whether that's by passing laws to save the environment or fighting for fair pay.

Politics was the right path for Alexandria to make a difference. She's inspired many young people, especially young women, to think about a future in politics for themselves. However, no matter what path you choose, you can find your own way to make a difference and to fight for causes you care about, just like Alexandria Ocasio-Cortez!

In Her Words

"There is no one person. This is the danger, the idea that any one person is going to save us is not true. I'm not going to save us. Only we can save us. And I'm only as useful or powerful as the amount of people knocking on doors and talking to their neighbors."

— Interview with *Elle* magazine from July 2018

Be Like
Alexandria Ocasio-Cortez!

If you use social media, use it in a way that builds people up and helps people learn more about causes you care about.

Volunteer in your community.

Speak out about issues that matter to you.

Run for student government at your school.

Do your part to help the environment, including recycling.

Write to your government leaders about problems you see in the world and ways you think they can be fixed.

Alexandria Ocasio-Cortez didn't listen to people who said she was too young to make a difference. You're not too young either! These are just some ways you can make a difference if you want to be like Alexandria.

GLOSSARY

accountable: Required to explain actions or choices.

affect: To produce an effect on something.

climate change: Change in Earth's weather caused by human activity.

compromise: To settle a disagreement by agreeing that each side will change or give up some of what it is asking for.

economy: The way in which goods and services are made, sold, and used in a country or area.

environment: The natural world around us.

immigrant: A person who comes to a country to live there.

inspire: To move someone to do something great.

represent: To act officially for someone or something.

revealing: Giving information that was not known before.

righteous: Following what is just or proper.

risk: The possibility that something bad will happen.

volunteer: To do something to help because you want to do it.

FOR MORE INFORMATION

WEBSITES

Ben's Guide to the U.S. Government

bensguide.gpo.gov

This website, which features different pages for different age groups, is a fun way to learn more about how the U.S. government works.

Congresswoman Alexandria Ocasio-Cortez

ocasio-cortez.house.gov

This is the official House of Representatives website for Alexandria Ocasio-Cortez.

BOOKS

Gonzales, Leticia. *Alexandria Ocasio-Cortez: Get to Know the Rising Politician*. North Mankato, MN: Capstone Press, 2020.

Leigh, Anna. *Alexandria Ocasio-Cortez: Political Headliner*. Minneapolis, MN: Lerner Publications, 2020.

Thomas, Rachael L. *Alexandria Ocasio-Cortez*. Minneapolis, MN: ABDO Publishing, 2020.

INDEX